Love

99 Ways To Show You Care

Stewart Ferris

summersdale

Summersdale Publishers Ltd
46 West Street
Chichester
West Sussex
PO19 1RP
UK

www.summersdale.com

Printed and bound in Great Britain.

ISBN 1 84024 400 3

1.

Say it with flowers.

Plant daffodil bulbs on waste ground on the approach to an airport runway, so that they spell 'I Love You'. Don't do this on an area that gets mowed. Wait until the spring, then send your lover up in a plane to view your message. Don't include a name in the message unless you already know someone by that name.

2.

Say it with chocolate.

Buying your lover a box of
chocolates sends a clear message
of affection. If your lover is on
a diet, however, you can send
the same cocoa love message
by giving them shares in
a chocolate company.

3.

Say it with a diary.

*Write your message in your
lover's diary so that it will
be discovered at some
point in the future.*

4.

Say it with a smile.

Using a non-toxic ink, write
'I Love You' across your teeth,
then smile at your lover,
revealing your message.
This doesn't work if you
have less than ten teeth.

5.

Say it under water.

Tap her face mask, offer her your oxygen supply, and synchronise your sub-aqua breathing as you share one oxygen tank. Your supply is limited, so take care not to breathe too heavily.

6.

Say it in the car.

Affix a note saying 'I Love You' to the sun visor. With your lover in the passenger seat, point the car towards the sun so they have to lower the visor and read your message. An alternative message might be, 'Would you like to borrow some sunglasses?'

7.

Say it on an aeroplane.

Find out where the microphone
is located, distract the crew, and
make the following announcement:
'Ladies and gentlemen, I would
like to announce that the recent
turbulence was due to [name] and
myself becoming members of the
Mile High Club.'

8.

Say it in a wallet.

Write your message on a Post-It note,
stick it to one of their credit cards,
and put it back in their wallet.
The next shop-keeper they meet
is going to be in for a surprise.

9.

Say it from behind.

Creep up behind your lover while they are performing their ablutions in front of the bathroom mirror, and hold up a sign over their shoulder on which is written(in reverse) your message, so that they can read it normally in the mirror.

10.

Say it by post.

Or a totem pole. Carve your
message in some kind of tall
stick and plant it in your lover's
garden as a beacon for your
feelings and an amenity
for local pets.

11.

Say it over breakfast.

Using magnetic letters that
stick to the fridge
and fall off if you slam
the door too hard.

12.

Say it on air.

Phone in to a live talk show on
your local radio station. Instead
of showing your ignorance of the
day's topic, like all the other callers,
quickly say your private message
before they cut you off for
making the show too interesting.

13.

Say it in the sand.

Carve your amorous message
in enormous letters by the sea,
then take a photo for posterity.
Try to make your message in
front of a prominent seaside
erection, such as a lighthouse.

14.

Say it with stamps.

Get a rubber printing stamp made
up with your message, then get a
job working at your lover's bank.
When they come to pay in some money, instead
of stamping the date on their paying in book,
stamp 'I love you' on it instead.
Remember to change the stamp before the
next customer arrives.

15.

Say it with fireworks.

This one requires an assistant.
Take your lover to a secluded
spot at night, with a view of a
nearby hill. At a pre-arranged
time the fireworks will explode
in the night sky above you.
State your message immediately
prior to this moment.

16.

Say it in front of Friends.

*While you're both watching an
episode of Friends, get up to turn
off the television. On your back
will be a piece of paper
with the message.*

17.

Say it with your feet.

This involves playing 'footsie' at a restaurant, to see how much titillation can be achieved using your foot under the table without anyone else noticing (apart from your lover, of course).

18.

Say it in music.

If the two of you have a 'special song', try to get it played on a radio station with your message. Failing that, just telephone your lover and play a love song into the ear-piece. Don't speak when the song has finished, just put the phone down.

19.

Say it permanently.

Scrape your message into wet
cement with your finger or a stick,
and embellish it with a palm print
so that the police will have
an easier job tracking you down.

20.

Say it in the nude.

Spend an evening naked together,
then confirm that despite the way
they look you still love them.

21.

Say it in a lift.

Take your lover to a tall building, and travel in
the lift to the top floor. When the doors open, a
banner displaying 'I Love You' (put there by
you earlier) will be the first thing they see.

22.

Say it in the window.

Affix your message to your lover's
bedroom window before you go to bed
and hide it behind the curtains.
When they open the curtains
in the morning your message will
be staring them in the face.

23.

Say it in a bottle.

Put your message in a bottle and throw it into the sea, where it will travel across the oceans for many years, and may one day be posted back to your lover with a letter complaining about how you littered the oceans.

24.

Say it with a
note under the pillow.

C# *is a nice one.*

25.

Say it with a go-between.

*Messages from third parties seem
more risqué and covert, especially
if your lover doesn't know them.
Time the delivery for maximum surprise,
usually when your lover is at work.*

26.

Say it in the car stereo.

Record your message on a CD or cassette
and put it in your lover's car so that it
will play when they next drive to work.

27.

Say it in public.

*Put an advert in the local paper
on any day of the year . . .
don't just wait for St Valentine's Day.*

28.

Say it with a poem.

Write an original love poem, or just copy out a
famous one in your own handwriting, then put it
in their pocket when they're not looking.
Use a permanent ink so that the poem will still
be legible after it's been through the wash.

29.

Say it in a card game.

Write 'I Love You' on one the cards
before the game, then wait for
the special card to turn up
during the game.

30.

Say it on a banner.

Paint your message onto a sheet and attach to a bridge over a road. When your lover drives beneath it, later in the morning, it will have been blown upside-down by the wind, rendering the message invisible.

31.

Say it in a movie.

*Record a video of a romantic film
and then film yourself in a
short scene at the end.*

32.

Say it in a book.

Slip a note into the book they are reading,
and hope they get to the last chapter
before lending it to a friend.

33.

Say it in Scrabble.

Don't leave it to chance, though . . .
take the letters you need before the
game starts and keep them in your
pocket until it's time to place
them casually on the board.

34.

Say it in the stars.

Take your lover to a hilltop on a clear night and
explain that one of the constellations spells
'I love you' in ancient Greek. Probably.

35.

Say it with a drink.

Not necessarily with a drink or two inside you
. . . go to a cocktail bar and order a
romantically named cocktail for your lover.

36.

Say it
with a part of your body.

Paint the message onto a part of
your body that is not normally
exposed, then expose it.

37.

Say it with a feather.

Tickle the words 'I love you' onto their back with a feather. It's difficult to decipher words written on you in this way, so make sure they don't misinterpret what you're trying to say as 'You're fat'.

38.

Say it on holiday.

Don't just say it in a romantic setting, but say it when you're both stressed, the flight is delayed, your luggage is missing, and you've been arguing about trivia. It will mean much more to say it out of context in this way.

39.

Say it in Morse code.

•• •——•• ——————— •••—— • ———•———

——————— ••——

40.

Say it with a pet.

*Not heavy petting, but if you have
a dog train it to carry a piece of
paper to your lover without eating it.*

41.

Say it with oil.

Cover your lover with massage oil from head to toe, then slowly massage every part of them.

42.

Say it with body language.

Let your lover into your 'personal space' and
make physical contact whenever possible.

43.

Say it with attention to detail.

*Simply noticing when your lover has had a
haircut and pretending it looks great
is enough to say you love them.*

44.

Say it at the funfair.

Go on a twisting ride by yourself,
while your lover watches.
As you hurtle past yell
out your message.
If this is too public, take your lover
to the top of the big wheel
and declare your love there.

45.

Say it in soap.

Carve your message in the underside of
their bar of soap, and leave it for
them to discover in the bath.

46.

Say it in the garden.

Attach notes to their lawn mower or
garden tools, or even stick them to plants
that you know are tended regularly.
Make sure they haven't recently
taken on a gardener, though.

47.

Say it in a blink.

Get someone to paint your
message onto your eyelids
so that when you close your
eyes it says 'I Love You',
then try not to fall asleep at work.

48.

Say it on a computer.

Sabotage your lover's computer so that the
screensaver reads 'I Love You'.
Better still, set up the 'wallpaper'
as a scanned image of the two of you.

49.

Say it on a map.

Write your message on a map next to a place name, then give the map to your lover and ask them to show you how best to get to that place.

50.

Say it in the oven.

Under the sign that says
'When are you going to clean this oven?'
add another note
that says 'I love you'.

51.

Say it on a picnic.

Prepare the picnic hamper yourself, and attach little messages to the items inside it. Make sure your lover is in charge of opening it up and sharing out the food.

52.

Say it by telephone.

Find out the number of a public telephone
booth, then secretly dial that number
from your mobile as you walk past it
with your lover. Suggest that they
answer the call, then tell
them your message.

53.

Say it with rubbish.

Attach your message to the
underside of a pedal bin.
When your lover throws away
the awful meal you cooked,
your message will appear.

54.

Say it in disguise.

Visit your lover at work or some place where you don't normally meet, and disguise yourself heavily. Start flirting with them, then tell them you love them and watch the reaction . . . it's best to reveal your identity quickly in case they react too positively to your amorous advances.

55.

Say it on a bicycle.

Hire a bicycle made for two, and sit in the
front seat. Once you have worked up a sweat,
remove a piece of clothing to reveal
your message stuck to your back.

56.

Say it in the shower.

Take a shower together, outdoors if
it's warm and private enough, and whisper
your message from beneath the streaming
warm water on your faces.

57.

Say it with hair.

Find out where your lover gets their hair cut and surreptitiously visit during their appointment. When the cut has been finished, trade places with the hairdresser and hold up the mirror, with 'I Love You' written in reverse on it. When viewed via the mirror in front it will make sense.

58.

Say it on the Internet.

Put up a web-page declaring your love,
and then get your lover to look themselves up on
the Internet to see what entries come up.
(Best to make sure yours is the
only one, before you do this.)

59.

Say it on the bathroom mirror.

With a greasy finger, wipe your
message onto your lover's bathroom
mirror. Next time the mirror
steams up, your message will appear.

60.

Say it on the moon.

Make a fake telescope, or remove the lenses from an old one. Write your message in thick letters on clear acetate film so that it takes up less space than the telescope's diameter, and attach it to the end of the telescope. When there is a clear night with a full moon, get your lover to look through the telescope at the moon. They will see your message 'written' on the moon.

61.

Say it with toilet paper.

Unroll the toilet paper in
your lover's bathroom, write
your message on one of the sheets,
then carefully roll it back up again.

62.

Say it in a parcel.

*If you have enough brown paper, wrap yourself
up and 'deliver' yourself to your lover's door.
Say your message when you are unwrapped.
Alternatively, wrap a small gift in several
layers, and between each layer include a note
with a part of your message.*

63.

Say it with a dart.

*Write your message on a piece of
paper prior to a game of darts
with your lover. During the game,
pin your message to one of your
darts and throw. Your message
will be automatically pinned to
the dartboard for all to see.*

64.

Say it on a shopping list.

Sabotage your lover's shopping
list by adding your message to it,
and perhaps one or two
love-making accessories.

65.

Say it with taste.

*Put a love heart sweet printed
with your message onto your tongue,
and then gently insert into
your lover's mouth.*

66.

Say it without taste.

*Give your lover a tasteless
little fluffy toy with your
message pre-printed onto its chest.*

67.

Say it in the washing machine.

*Leave a note in your lover's
washing machine so that it
reveals itself next time they pull
out the tray to put in some powder.*

68.

Say it with a shaver.

Carefully shave a part of your
lover's body to reveal your message.

69.

Say in the past.

Bury your message in an old tin,
then dig it up in front of your
lover whilst 'gardening'.
It's best to use old-looking paper,
so that it looks as if the whole
thing had been buried fifty years ago.

70.

Say it with a mobile phone.

Some mobile phones can be programmed to display a personalised message when you switch it on. Do this to your lover's phone so that your message appears next time they switch it on.

71.

Say it with pizza.

Create a pizza that spells out your
message using the various toppings,
and cook it for your lover.

72.

Say it with balloons.

Learn balloon bending techniques and bend some long, thin balloons together so that they spell out your message. Alternatively, blow up a balloon, pinch the end, and write your message on it in small letters. When you let the air out, your message will 'disappear', ready to reappear as if by magic when you blow it up in front of your lover.

73.

Say it with a hat.

*Lift your hat to your lover when
they walk by, revealing your
message on its underside.*

74.

Say it with a shoe.

Write your message on a piece of paper,
then screw it up into a ball and place it inside your
lover's shoe. Much to their annoyance,
they will be able to feel the paper when
they put the shoe on. Your message
should assuage their frustration.

75.

Say it with a long rod.

*Take your lover on a fishing trip,
and pretend to catch a pre-prepared 'fish'
consisting of an object with your
message written on it.*

76.

Say it on a golf course.

Take your lover for a round of golf.
Write your message on a ball,
then swap it for their ball
after they have putted it.

77.

Say it at the theatre.

Join a local amateur dramatics company with
your lover, and get parts as lovers in a
production. You may get to speak your message
in front of hundreds of people.

78.

Say it anonymously.

Cut and paste your message from pieces of newsprint, in the style of an anonymous ransom note, then post it to your lover.

79.

Say it window cleaning.

Clean one of your lover's windows, either on
their house or on the car, while your lover
watches from inside. Smear soapy water all
over the glass, then scrape clean
(in reverse) your message.

80.

Say it with suction.

Write your note on a piece of paper and place it inside the nozzle of your lover's vacuum cleaner so that it jams it up and prevents suction. When your lover attempts to hoover they will inspect the blockage and discover your message. Of course, a better way to demonstrate your love would be to do the vacuum cleaning yourself.

81.

Say it at a wedding.

Especially when it's your own.

82.

Say it in the middle of the night.

Wake up your lover purely
to tell them your message.
This is less popular if you do
it from a great distance.

83.

Say it in a crossword.

Prepare a private crossword game
for your lover which reveals your
message if the clues are
correctly interpreted.

84.

Say it with red roses.

*A bunch of red roses delivered to your lover is
the most traditional way to say 'I love you'
(other than actually just saying it, of course).*

85.

Say it with a kite.

Attach your message to the kite string so that it flies in the air beneath the kite, then fly the contraption outside your lover's window.

86.

Say it with an echo.

Next time you happen to be in a rocky valley, shout your message so that it echoes for miles around. Alternatively, rent a public address system, switch the reverb level to maximum, and declare your love.

87.

Say it with a musician.

If an itinerant musician should
visit your restaurant while you're dining,
don't just call the police: bribe the musician to
play a special song dedicated to your lover.
Then call the police.

88.

Say it with snow.

Write your message in the snow outside your lover's bedroom window so that it will be the first thing they see when they look out of the window in the morning.

89.

Say it in a whisper.

Whisper your message to your lover when they
least expect it, such as in a supermarket queue
or when they've been stopped for speeding.

90.

Say it with a Jack-in-the-Box.

Attach your message to the head of a Jack-in-
the-Box, and give it to your lover to open.

91.

Say it with resolution.

Make it your New Year's resolution to tell your
partner that you love them in a
different way every day.

92.

Say it in mid-conversation.

For no apparent reason, interrupt your lover in mid-conversation and tell them that you love them.

93.

Say it on a parking ticket.

Create a fake parking ticket on which is written your message, then stick it to the windscreen of your lover's car.

94.

Say it with a kiss.

But don't talk with your mouth full.

95.

Say it with a tattoo.

Preferably one that washes
off after you sober up.

96.

Say it over dinner.

Make sure you go somewhere
that serves Alphabetti Spaghetti.

97.

Say it in bed.

. . . to the nurse when she comes
to empty your bedpan.

98.

Say it with a puppet.

Buy a ventriloquist's dummy and use
it to say your message for you
(while you drink a glass of water).

99.

Say it with a hug.

A hug says it all. There's no need to speak.